THE
POWER
OF
YOUR WORDS

THE
POWER
OF
YOUR WORDS

by

Billy Joe Daugherty

The Power of Your Words
ISBN 1-56267-197-9
Copyright © 2000 by
Billy Joe Daugherty
Victory Christian Center
7700 South Lewis Avenue
Tulsa, OK 74136-7700

CONTENTS

INTRODUCTION

Your words have awesome power. God created the worlds with His words: **"And God said. . . ." "And God said. . . ." "And God said. . . ."** What He spoke came into being. In fact, everything God created came into being as a result of His words, which are filled with authority and power.

As a born-again child of God, you have been given authority because of Jesus' death, burial, and resurrection. Jesus has given us an example of how to overcome the devil and his works with the spoken Word.

In this book, *The Power of Your Words,* my goal is to get you to *believe* and *speak* God's Word as your standard for life and as a lifestyle rather than it being something you do just when you're in a crisis. You will avoid many of the crises of life or readily overcome them as you learn the value of the spoken Word of God coming through your lips.

My wife Sharon helps me in teaching chapter 3, "You Are Eating Your Words!" Together we examine the Word and verify it with personal experiences of how to submit your tongue – a small but unruly member of your body – to the control of the Holy Spirit.

You can change the course of your life by the words you are speaking. If your destiny needs an adjustment, take a critical look at what you have been speaking, and ask the Holy Spirit, the Helper, to help you speak only what God says about you and about others.

Billy Joe Daugherty

1

"Once you get a revelation of the power of your words and begin to align your words with God's Word, you can absolutely change your life forever."

Billy Joe Daugherty

1

THE AWESOME POWER
OF OUR WORDS

The Scriptures reveal the awesome power of our words.
Proverbs 18:20,21 KJV says:

> **A man's belly shall be satisfied with the fruit of his**
> **mouth; and with the increase of his lips shall he be filled.**

> **Death and life are in the power of the tongue: and**
> **they that love it shall eat the fruit thereof.**

In verses 4, 7, 8, and 13 KJV of this same chapter, the
power of our words – either as a positive or as a negative
force – is revealed:

> **The words of a man's mouth are as deep waters, and**
> **the wellspring of wisdom as a flowing brook . . .**

> **A fool's mouth is his destruction, and his lips are the**
> **snare of his soul.**

> **The words of a talebearer are as wounds, and they**
> **go down into the innermost parts of the belly . . .**

> **He that answereth a matter before he heareth it, it is**
> **folly and shame unto him.**

When we look at these verses, we can see the awesome power of words – how our words can wound and

hurt, or how they can be like a wellspring of life, pouring forth the wisdom of God. Our words can bring shame, or they can bring honor. They can edify or they can condemn.

Verse 20 KJV says, **"A man's belly shall be satisfied with the fruit of his mouth . . . ."** So what is "the *fruit* of your mouth"? It is the words that you are speaking.

Have you ever heard the phrase, "You are going to eat your words"? Here's a revelation for you. *You have been eating your words all of your life!* You are being satisfied right now in your life by the words that you are speaking.

Everything we do will bring a harvest of like kind according to the law of seedtime and harvest. Our thoughts, words, and actions are seeds which will produce a harvest. You are eating your words every day. When you speak blessing, you reap blessing. If you decree life, you will reap life. If you are speaking joy, peace, triumph, and victory, you will reap a harvest of joy, peace, triumph, and victory.

When you are born again through faith in Jesus Christ, you have authority to release the power of God's Word through your lips. His angels hearken to His Word. God watches over His Word to perform it. (Jeremiah 1:12.) God's Word is like a hammer. **" 'Is not My word like a fire?' says the Lord, 'and like a hammer that breaks the rock in pieces?' "** (Jeremiah 23:29). It's like a sword.

4

It will destroy the works of the enemy. It will also bring health, strength, and life to you or to those over whom you are praying God's Word.

Proverbs 4:22 says this about God's words: **"They are *life* unto those who find them, and *health* to all their flesh."**

Once you get a revelation of the power of your words and begin to align your words with God's Word, you can absolutely change your life forever. You are eating and walking and living in the fruit of your own lips.

Accountable for "Idle" Words

Do you need to change some of the words you are speaking? Have you ever used any of these phrases?

- Dead sure.

- Dying to get there.

- Afraid so.

Is it any wonder people are plagued with fear and death? You may be thinking, *But those are just idle words.* Wait a minute! Jesus said we would give account of every idle word that we speak:

> **But I say to you that for every idle word men may speak, they will give account of it in the day of judgment.**

> **For by your words you will be justified, and by your
> words you will be condemned.**
>
> **Matthew 12:36,37**

Idle words, just like faith-filled words, do have an
effect and they will bring a harvest. The enemy has sown
words of fear and death, torment and oppression into the
language of people so that many people are constantly
speaking disaster, calamity, tragedy, and heaviness. Their
mouth is so accustomed to speaking negatively they don't
even think about it. It comes directly from their heart out
of their mouth, and they are walking out their own words.

> **A good man out of the good treasure of his heart
> brings forth good things, and an evil man out of the evil
> treasure brings forth evil things.**
>
> **Matthew 12:35**

This is a spiritual principle that works whether you
understand it or not.

Jesus Defeated the Devil with
the Sword of the Word

The devil understands the power of words, because
when he challenged Jesus in Matthew, chapter 4, Jesus
pulled the sword of the Word on him. He didn't wave a
Bible. Jesus just took the sword, put it in His own mouth,
and spoke it: IT IS WRITTEN.

Let's look at verses 1-11 in Matthew, chapter 4, to get a better understanding of the power of Jesus' words that defeated the devil's temptations and ran him off. Remember, Jesus is our example for defeating the devil and running him off, too.

Then Jesus was led up by the Spirit into the wilderness to be tempted by the devil.

And when He had fasted forty days and forty nights, afterward He was hungry.

Now when the tempter came to Him, he said, "If You are the Son of God, command that these stones become bread."

But He answered and said, *"It is written,* 'Man shall not live by bread alone, but by every word that proceeds from the mouth of God.'"

Then the devil took Him up into the holy city, set Him on the pinnacle of the temple,

And said to Him, "If You are the Son of God, throw Yourself down. For it is written: 'He shall give His angels charge over you,' and 'In their hands they shall bear you up, lest you dash your foot against a stone.'"

Jesus said to him, *"It is written again,* 'You shall not tempt the Lord your God.'"

Again, the devil took Him up on an exceedingly high mountain, and showed Him all the kingdoms of the world and their glory.

> And he said to Him, "All these things I will give You if You will fall down and worship me."
>
> Then Jesus said to him, "Away with you, Satan! For it is written, 'You shall worship the Lord your God, and Him only you shall serve.' "
>
> Then the devil left Him, and behold, angels came and ministered to Him.

The spoken Word of God through Jesus' lips stopped the devil. The spoken Word of God through your lips will stop him, too.

The armor of God is defined in Ephesians 6:10-18, and in that list of armor is "the sword of the Spirit," which is the Word of God. It is the spoken Word of God (rhema) that is your weapon against the enemy. The devil knows and understands that.

To the degree that you speak the Word of God, you will defeat the devil. By your words you will release the blessings of God and start walking in the abundance He has for you. Many people confess tragedy and accidents. They say they are an accident going somewhere to happen. (I never ride with anyone who says that!)

Reprogramming Yourself with God's Word

The power of your words is revealed throughout the entire Bible. What would happen if you changed your conversation to line up with God's Word? What would happen if you would begin to talk like Jesus?

This is the day the Lord has made. I will rejoice and be glad in it. The Lord is my Shepherd, I shall not want. The Lord is my refuge and my fortress. No evil will befall me and no plague can come near my dwelling. I can do all things through Christ who strengthens me.

What would happen if you would program your mind, your heart, and your lips with God's Word? What you believe, think, and speak will be fulfilled in your life.

Stop the Death Talk!

Sharon and I have witnessed many situations where people received exactly what they were speaking – tragedies, trials, and calamities. I'm talking about Spirit-filled Christians.

There are people who pray and sing one thing in church, but their prayers, songs, and words are the exact opposite when they go home. If you've got one stream going one way and one going the opposite way, they are negating each other. It's double-mindedness. If we are going to sing that we have the victory, then let's talk the victory every day. If you sing, "I will live and not die," let's talk life every day. If we are going to sing that God always causes us to triumph, then let's say it every day: *God always causes me to triumph.*

It's up to you and me to make a choice to stop the death talk. **"Death and life are in the power of the tongue, and those who love it will eat its fruit"** (Proverbs 18:21). We are eating the fruit of our words.

Remember, the seed of your words is planted first, then comes the harvest. Most people want the harvest first, then they will plant the seed. That's true in finances as well as in confession. Some people say, "Well, I'm not living in victory right now. How can I say I'm walking in victory?" You have to plant the seed of victory with your words first.

Someone might say that they're not living in peace. How can they say they have the peace of God? It all depends on whether you believe your feelings more than the Word of God. It all depends on whether you believe your circumstances more than the Word of God. If you believe what others say about you more than what the Word of God says, then you will just keep on saying the negative, ungodly things and you'll live them out in your life.

The good news is, if you believe that God's Word is greater than the circumstances, greater than your feelings, greater than the opinions and reports of others, then you can start saying, *I am redeemed. I am blessed. I am a new creation in Christ Jesus. All things are working together for good in my life.* Glory to God! Let God arise and let His enemies be scattered!

You can begin to speak over your home, *The blessings of God abide in this place.* You create the atmosphere of your home with your own words. Potpourri has no authority over devils! A house that's filled with gloom and strife is going to require more than strawberry or fresh spring blossom scents to drive them away!

Today is your day to make a decision, *I'm going to fill my heart with God's Word, I will speak His Word, and with the help of the Holy Spirit, I will align my words and thoughts with the sword of the Spirit (God's Word)!*

2

"*Your tongue may be very small, but it guides your whole life.*"

Billy Joe Daugherty

2

BRIDLING THE TONGUE

In the New Testament, James devoted an entire chapter to the power of our words. In verse 2 of James, chapter 3, he says:

> **For we all stumble in many things. If anyone does not stumble in word, he is a perfect man, able also to bridle the whole body.**

The word "perfect" means complete or full of age.[1] Webster defines "perfect" as being entirely without fault or defect; accurate; faithfully reproducing the original; pure; mature.[2]

A person who has his words under control is a mature believer, able to control his whole body.

Did you know that your mouth can control your eating habits? If you get your tongue under control and you begin to speak, "I'm not going to overeat today," you can begin

---

[1]James Strong. "Greek Dictionary of the New Testament," The New Strong's Exhaustive Concordance of the Bible (Nashville, TN: Thomas Nelson Publishers, 1995), p. 90, #5046.

[2]Merriam Webster's Collegiate Dictionary, Tenth Ed. (Springfield, MA: Merriam-Webster, Inc., 1996), p. 862.

to rule your body and tell it what it's going to do. You can tell your body what weight it is going to be. With the help of the Holy Spirit, you will achieve and maintain that goal.

Many people say, "I lose a little and then I gain it all back." Guess what happens? Exactly what they are saying. Begin to say, "I am eating right. My body is under the control of the Holy Spirit. I exercise daily." James says *you can control, or bridle, your whole body with the words of your mouth.* Obviously we must do the Word we are speaking for it to have an effect in our lives.

Some people say they can't stop sinning or they can't break a certain habit. They say it because they think it and believe it. Guess what? They continue to live in sin, even though they confess to be a believer and they go to church regularly.

Their primary source of bondage is in the words that are being spoken from their own mouth. Death and life are in the power of the tongue. If the devil can keep you reinforcing the thing that has you bound with your own words, you will not be liberated from it. Begin to believe and speak that Jesus broke the power of sin and that He gave you the victory over sin through His death, burial, and resurrection.

Jesus said, **"If the Son makes you free, you shall be free indeed"** (John 8:36). That means to be *totally free.* Begin to declare, *I am free from every filthy habit, and I am free from every tormenting thought, in Jesus' name.*

16

Repeated Applications of God's Word Are Needed!

You may be wondering, *What if a wrong thought comes back?* Speak the Word again.

What do you do if bugs come to your house? When Sharon and I were first married, we lived in a little garage apartment that seemed like it was built shortly after the Civil War! We used all types of spray to fight an invasion of bugs. The lady who lived next door in a little garage apartment leaned out her door one day and said, "Are you kids fighting bugs?" I said, "Yes, ma'am." She said, "Well, they are all coming over here. But that's okay. I'll fight them, too, and we'll send them back to the lady behind us!"

So what do you do if another bug shows up? You keep spraying. You keep fighting them. What do you do if a wrong feeling comes back, a wrong attitude persists, or a temptation comes? You don't say, "Oh, well, I tried to resist once, but it just didn't work." No, you keep fighting by quoting the Word. You keep *believing* and *speaking* the promises of God's Word.

Remember the old hymn, "Standing on the Promises"? It says to take the promises of God, believe them, confess them, and stand on them in faith until you see them manifested in your life. So this isn't some newfound revelation.

This goes all the way back to the very beginning of people believing the Word of God, like Abraham and Noah.

Whichever Way Your Tongue Goes, You Will Go!

In James 3:3-5, James says:

Indeed, we put bits in horses' mouths that they may obey us, and we turn their whole body.

Look also at ships: although they are so large and are driven by fierce winds, they are turned by a very small rudder wherever the pilot desires.

Even so the tongue is a little member and boasts great things. See how great a forest a little fire kindles!

James compares your tongue to the bit in a horse's mouth and to the rudder on a ship. Whichever way the captain of the ship turns the small rudder, the massive ship which weighs tons will turn.

It's the same way with a horse. You can put a 45-pound ten year old on a 1,500-pound horse. If the child knows how to hold on to the reins and pull the bit, he will control the horse and turn him where he wants him to go.

James is saying exactly the same thing that Solomon said in Proverbs 18:21: **"Death and life are in the power of the tongue. . . ."** Whichever way the tongue goes, that's the way your whole life will go. If your life is going the wrong way, take hold of the reins. Take hold of the controls of the ship of your life with the little member which is right below your nose and above your chin! Your tongue is the bit. It's the rudder. It's the governor or the control of your whole life. Take the Word of God that you have read and fit it to your lips. Release the power of life every day over your own life and over the lives of others by speaking what God says.

Taking Dominion with Your Words

God created you to take dominion. The devil doesn't have authority over any part of your life. Take charge in every area and tell the devil he has no place. Define the type of atmosphere that you want to prevail in your home and workplace.

Jesus said:

> **Assuredly, I say to you, whatever you bind on earth will be bound in heaven, and whatever you loose on earth will be loosed in heaven.**
>
> **Matthew 18:18**

Job 22:28 KJV says, **"Thou shalt also decree a thing, and it shall be established unto thee. . . ."** *You* have dominion and authority to decree a thing.

James goes on to say:

And the tongue is a fire, a world of iniquity. The tongue is so set among our members that it defiles the whole body, and sets on fire the course of nature; and it is set on fire by hell.

For every kind of beast and bird, of reptile and creature of the sea, is tamed and has been tamed by mankind.

But no man can tame the tongue. It is an unruly evil, full of deadly poison.

With it we bless our God and Father, and with it we curse men, who have been made in the similitude of God.

Out of the same mouth proceed blessing and cursing. My brethren, these things ought not to be so.

Does a spring send forth fresh water and bitter from the same opening?

Can a fig tree, my brethren, bear olives, or a grapevine bear figs? Thus no spring yields both salt water and fresh.

James 3:6-12

James says, **"No man can tame the tongue"** (v. 8). However, he doesn't discount the work of the Holy Spirit in developing a tongue that is under His control!

In Matthew 12:34 Jesus said, **"Out of the abundance of the heart the mouth speaks."** In Mark 11:23 He said:

For assuredly, I say to you, whoever says to this mountain, "Be removed and be cast into the sea," and

**does not doubt in his heart, but believes that those things
he says will be done, he will have whatever he says.**

For you to believe that the Word spoken from your lips
has authority, you have to get to the point that you believe
everything you say is going to come to pass. Your heart
will not be in agreement with you if you are constantly
joking or bad-mouthing.

Begin each day by asking the Holy Spirit to bridle your
tongue:

**Set a guard, O Lord, over my mouth; keep watch
over the door of my lips.**

Psalm 141:3

3

From the fruit of his mouth a man's stomach is filled; with the harvest from his lips he is satisfied.

Proverbs 18:20 NIV

3

YOU ARE EATING YOUR WORDS!

Billy Joe & Sharon Daugherty

Billy Joe:

> The words of the wicked are, "Lie in wait for blood,"
> but *the mouth of the upright will deliver them.*
>
> **Proverbs 12:6**

This verse gives us a contrast. The words of the wicked are destructive and violent, but the words of the righteous – those who are in right standing with God, who are serving Him and pursuing Him – will deliver them. The words of the wicked are planning attack, evil, disaster, calamity, and tragedy toward people. But the words of the righteous will bring deliverance and encouragement to you and to others.

Have you ever heard the statement that someone has put their foot in their mouth? They said something that wasn't edifying and it caused problems. Let's turn it around. We can put the right foot forward by speaking right words that agree with God's Word. There is awesome power in your words.

Sharon:

Back in 1974 when we first began to hear the message of the power of our words, I began to memorize Psalm 91. David the psalmist had an understanding of the power of his words, because throughout the psalms he said, "I will say." In Psalm 91, a psalm most of us are familiar with, he says:

> **He who dwells in the secret place of the Most High shall abide under the shadow of the Almighty.**
>
> *I will say of the Lord,* "He is my refuge and my fortress; my God, in Him I will trust."
>
> **Verses 1,2**

A girl in our youth group wanted to jog with me through our neighborhood which I did regularly. Since she jogged faster than I did, she was ahead of me. I was meditating on Psalm 91 and speaking it out of my mouth as I jogged.

Suddenly, a man walked out of his little house in this neighborhood. He had a gun in his hand and he pointed it at me, just walking forward with a dazed look. I'm running in the street, and I began to pray in tongues. I turned into a parking lot that was to one side, because he would have had full aim at me if I turned the other direction.

I kept quoting these verses from Psalm 91. I heard a click behind me. Nothing happened. I ran back to my house and waited on the girl who had already gone around the block.

When she got back to our house, I said, "Do you know who lives in that house?" She said, "That guy was shell-shocked in war. He has to be watched by his parents. He stays at his house all the time and usually they keep him inside."

I said, "Well, he got out! He came out of his house with a real gun, and I heard a click." I said, "I have been memorizing Psalm 91 and praying that over my life. I just believe the angels protected me and that there wasn't a bullet in that slot for the gun to go off at me."

I was thinking, *My words delivered me even before he came out of the house!*

Billy Joe:

Proverbs, chapter 12, verse 14, says, **"A man will be satisfied with good by the fruit of his mouth. . . ."** Over in the New Testament Jesus said:

> **Out of the abundance of the heart the mouth speaks.**
>
> **A good man out of the good treasure of his heart brings forth good things, and an evil man out of the evil treasure brings forth evil things.**
>
> **But I say to you that for every idle word men may speak, they will give account of it in the day of judgment.**

> **For by your words you will be justified, and by your words you will be condemned.**
>
> **Matthew 12:34-37**

God watches over His Word to perform it in behalf of those who believe and confess it. (See Jeremiah 1:12.)

Authority and power are released with your words. When you call a pizza company, you order pizza with your words. A delivery is made to your house based on the words you have spoken. There are similarities in the natural and spiritual realms. Every day we use words to release the blessings of God or to stop them. You will be satisfied with the fruit of your own words.

Sharon:

Psalm 103:20 KJV says:

> **Bless the Lord, ye his angels, that excel in strength, that do his commandments, hearkening unto the voice of his word.**

The angels of God are listening for God's words to be spoken from your mouth in the atmosphere around you. So as you speak what God says in His Word and you believe it, then the angels hearken to those words to perform them.

Billy Joe:

Have you ever heard someone say:

- I'm dead sure.

- I'm dying to get there.

- I'm an accident looking for a place to happen.

- My whole life is messed up continually.

You are projecting your future by the words you are speaking right now. We understand the principle of a farmer planting seeds and reaping the harvest on the seeds he has sown. We can sow the seeds of our finances, our time, of service, kindness, and goodness. But the seeds of our words grow and bring a harvest, too.

You are being satisfied or dissatisfied right now by the words of your mouth. If you're not happy with the way your life is presently, change the words that you are speaking and you will change your future. Hallelujah!

You can have a crop failure on bad seeds you have sown through *repentance.* Repentance requires confession. We confess our sins to God and He forgives our sin and cleanses us from all unrighteousness. (See 1 John 1:9.) Then we are released. Once you do that, begin to pray Psalm 51:10 over yourself: *Create in me a clean heart, O God, and renew a steadfast spirit within me.*

Psalm 51 is a confession that came from the psalmist David after his sins of adultery and murder were revealed by the prophet Nathan. The only way to get sin out is to reach down in your heart with your tongue and lay it out on the table before God, just as David did in this psalm:

Have mercy upon me, O God, according to Your lovingkindness; according to the multitude of Your tender mercies, blot out my transgressions.

Wash me thoroughly from my iniquity, and cleanse me from my sin.

For I acknowledge my transgressions, and my sin is always before me.

Against You, You only, have I sinned, and done this evil in Your sight – that You may be found just when You speak, and blameless when You judge.

Behold, I was brought forth in iniquity, and in sin my mother conceived me.

Behold, You desire truth in the inward parts, and in the hidden part You will make me to know wisdom.

Purge me with hyssop, and I shall be clean; wash me, and I shall be whiter than snow.

Make me hear joy and gladness, that the bones You have broken may rejoice.

Hide Your face from my sins, and blot out all my iniquities.

Create in me a clean heart, O God, and renew a steadfast spirit within me.

Do not cast me away from Your presence, and do not take Your Holy Spirit from me.

Restore to me the joy of Your salvation, and uphold me by Your generous Spirit.

Then I will teach transgressors Your ways, and sinners shall be converted to You.

Verses 1-13

The key to causing a crop failure on bad words you have spoken is called "confession of sin." Many times people just want to sweep it under the rug, not think about it, forget about it, but God requires that we confess it and forsake it. Only then are we forgiven and cleansed.

Begin to speak: *In the way of righteousness is life, and in its pathway there is no death. The Lord is my Shepherd, I shall not want.* (Proverbs 12:28; Psalm 23:1.)

Many people have been schooled their whole life to speak negatively. They talk about their family illnesses. "My grandmother and my mother had this problem." Then they say, "I'll probably have it too." Or, "Everyone in our family always gets this particular illness at this time of the year." They are snared with their own words. (Proverbs 6:2.)

Begin your day with a positive confession: *This is the day the Lord has made. I am going to rejoice and be glad in it. Everything my hand touches prospers.* (Psalm 118:24;

31

Deuteronomy 28:8.) Or, you can get up in the morning and say, "Good Lord, it's morning!" You set your table with the words you are speaking!

Sharon:

Years ago I had a friend living in an apartment in Tulsa. This friend's next door neighbor was negative about everything. There was a big tree in front of their apartment. Every now and then storms would come through Tulsa, and the neighbor lady would say, "One of these days that tree is going to fall on this apartment."

My friend said, "Not on this side. I bind those words in Jesus' name." Of course the lady didn't quite understand my friend who was a real positive person.

One day a storm with high winds came through Tulsa and my friend's neighbor got just what she had been confessing: The tree fell on her apartment!

Billy Joe:

This woman had been calling on that tree for years, just like calling the dog! She was snared with the words of her own mouth.

What we are talking about is more than having a positive or a negative attitude about life. The real issue is *speaking faith-filled words* – words that are in agreement with the Word of God. You believe the Word with your heart and speak it out with your mouth. So our foundation is the Word of God, our connection to it is faith, and the release of it is in the confession of our lips.

Sharon:

We need to understand the seriousness of our words, for our words are a matter of life and death.

I remember a situation years ago of a person who was always in a hurry. She said, "You know, one of these days I'm just going to kill myself driving as fast as I do." The day came when it happened. I thought to myself, *She spoke her destiny and didn't even realize it.*

Today if I hear someone say that or something similar, I'll say, "No, let's believe God that you are going to live and not die."

When you speak death words, divorce words, or words like, "He's a good for nothing . . . He'll never amount to anything . . . He'll never be free . . . It just seems like we never have enough . . . We'll never get out of this," you are digging a ditch and eventually you'll fall into it – unless there is repentance and a turnaround in what you are speaking.

Billy Joe:

How many children have been wounded by the negative words of a parent, a teacher, or someone else? They have lived with the stamp of "worthless" on their life. "You're going to wind up in prison." "You'll never amount to anything." Those words get down into a person's mind and heart. The only thing that can cancel them is the power of the Word of God and the work of the Holy Ghost.

If a child, a young person, or even an adult doesn't have the Word and the Holy Spirit to counter those words, they will sink to the level of the words spoken over them. They will become bitter or wounded or they will embrace and accept them and live at the level of the words spoken over them.

Remember, our heavenly Father has spoken good words over us. He says:

> **"For I know the plans I have for you," declares the Lord, "plans to prosper you and not to harm you, plans to give you hope and a future."**
>
> **Jeremiah 29:11 NIV**

> **You, dear children, are from God and have overcome them, because the one who is in you is greater than the one who is in the world.**
>
> **1 John 4:4 NIV**

Never will I leave you; never will I forsake you.
Hebrews 13:5 NIV

Let's tie these verses in with Second Corinthians 4:13. It gives a revelation on what we're talking about. This isn't a mind over matter issue, or pulling yourself up by your own bootstraps, or trying to have a positive attitude. We're talking about *believing* what God says rather than the opinions of other people, our own feelings, the circumstances, the latest news report or financial forecast.

Second Corinthians 4:13 says:

And since we have the same spirit of faith, according to what is written, "I *believed and therefore I spoke*," we also *believe* and therefore *speak*.

So the spirit of faith is based upon *believing* and *speaking* God's Word.

What we are talking about is, on every issue you face – your day, your future, your marriage, your family, your finances, health, victory, whatever – God has something to say about it. He has spoken in His Word revelation of His will for our lives. Every day we have a choice to make whether we are going to speak how we feel about things, how others view them, or what God says about them.

Moses put it this way:

I call heaven and earth as witnesses today against you, that I have set before you life and death, blessing

and cursing: therefore *choose life*, that both you and your descendants may live.

Deuteronomy 30:19

How do you make that choice? By *believing* and *speaking* the Word of God. When you begin to believe something and speak it, you will begin to act it out.

Sharon:

Joshua 1:8 says:

This Book of the Law shall not depart from your mouth, but you shall meditate in it day and night, that you may observe to do according to all that is written in it. For then you will make your way prosperous, and then you will have good success.

There are three things in this Scripture that we are to do:

- Do not let the Word depart out of your mouth.

- Meditate on the Word day and night.

- Observe to do (obey) *all* that is written in the Word.

In Proverbs 4:20 KJV God says, **"Attend to my words."** When you "tend" to something, you give it your attention. Verses 20-23 KJV go on to say:

Incline thine ear unto my sayings.

Let them not depart from thine eyes; keep them in the midst of thine heart.

For they are life unto those that find them, and health to all their flesh.

Keep thy heart with all diligence; for out of it are the issues of life.

If you are putting God's Word inside of you, it's going to come out of your mouth. What's in your heart is going to come out of your mouth. You are going to talk about it. This is why it's so important to guard the things you are seeing and hearing. Give attention to putting the Word of God in you so it will come out of your mouth.

Verse 24 of Proverbs, chapter 4, KJV says, **"Put away from thee a froward mouth, and perverse lips put far from thee."** "Froward" means to be disobedient. We could say, "Put away a disobedient mouth." Solomon wouldn't have said that if it wasn't possible to have a disobedient mouth.

When Billy Joe and I first heard this message, we began to watch our conversation, which we had not done prior to that time. We had watched our conversation as far as we didn't curse, but we had some negative words in our vocabulary that we didn't even think about.

Some people think it is bondage, but Solomon, inspired by the Spirit of God, said our words are *life* and *health* to all our flesh.

When you start helping someone else watch their words, you've got to be willing to be corrected, too.

When we were youth pastors, Billy Joe and I went out to eat with some of the youth after service one night. The guy who was sitting next to Billy Joe ordered spaghetti. As the waitress came near our table, she said, "Watch out, I'm going to spill this spaghetti on you." That's exactly what she said. Billy Joe said, "What?" and when his elbow went down, the plate of spaghetti flipped and went all over his suit!

Billy Joe:

I said, "Well, you said you were going to do it!" At least she announced it!

That incident awakened us and caused us to think about and listen to what people were saying and then watch what came to pass in their life.

We began to think about how people confess over their children that when they get to be teenagers, they are going to be wild and go away from God. We even heard Christians making those types of confessions. That's not in the Bible, but we realized it had been schooled into people's hearts by what they had seen happen in the world. We also realized that we had a choice about what we would speak over our children.

Sharon:

Another problem is that many times people speak fear words over their children to the point that their children live in fear. They can't even walk out of the house without being afraid. I've watched that with people. There is a soberness and a cautiousness that we need to have, because we are living in a perverse generation. The Bible has prophesied that it would be a time of gross darkness in the generation we are living in. We know by the continual negative newscasts that many bad things are going on.

Yet, on the other side of the coin, we are living in a wonderful time of the outpouring of God's Spirit. You can either focus on the bad or you can focus on the good. Be sober, alert, and sensitive to your spirit, but do not speak fear words.

Years ago I said to Billy Joe one day, "You need to wear a coat or you are going to catch a cold." He said, "You don't have to confess a cold over me. Just say, 'You need to wear a coat.'"

Sometimes when we went to see my parents, they would say, "Be careful." Billy Joe would say, "For nothing."

Billy Joe:

First Peter 5:7 says, **"Casting all your care upon Him, for He cares for you."** Why should we be full of cares when the Bible says we are to cast them on the Lord? Many people are full of cares, burdened, heavy laden, worried, and anxious.

Proverbs 12:6 says, **"The mouth of the upright will deliver them."** In other words, what you are speaking will either get you *in* trouble or *out* of trouble. Proverbs 14:3 says, **"The lips of the wise will preserve them."** Another word for "preserve" is to guard. He who guards his mouth guards his life.

Just a few months ago, one of the sons of my secretary attended services in the Mabee Center, along with his wife and children. At the time he was working for the State Department in the Embassy in Nairobi, Kenya.

Right after he and his family returned to Kenya, the Embassies in Tanzania and Nairobi were bombed, much like the Oklahoma City bombing. Many people were killed and hundreds more were hospitalized.

Glen Wells called his parents, Florence and Bill Wells in Tulsa, and said he had been in his office, but he was called upstairs to a meeting in an area of the building where he had not been before. The bomb hit when he was up-stairs, and his office was blown away. Three of the people who worked for him were killed. He was sorrowful for the loss of their lives but grateful he had been preserved.

For years his parents, Bill and Florence, have prayed

Psalm 91 over their sons and their families and they still do.

Here is a personalized version of Psalm 91 which you can pray over your children, over your own life, or over the lives of others:

My children dwell in the secret place of the Most High and they abide under the shadow of the Almighty. The Lord is their Refuge and Fortress, in Him they trust.

God will deliver my children from the snare of the fowler and from the perilous pestilence [the enemy and his traps, temptations, and snares], *in Jesus' name.*

God will cover them with His feathers and under His wings they will take refuge. His truth is their shield and buckler.

They will not be afraid of the terror by night, of the arrow that flies by day, of the pestilence that walks in darkness, nor of the destruction that lays waste at noonday.

A thousand may fall at their side and ten thousand at their right hand, but it will not come near them.

Because they have made the Lord their refuge and dwelling place, no evil will befall them nor will any plague come near them. He will give His angels charge over them to keep them in all their ways. The angels will bear them up. The enemy and his works they will trample underfoot.

Because my children set their love upon the Lord, He will deliver them and set them on high because they know His name. They will call upon the Lord and He will answer them. The Lord will be with them in trouble and He will deliver them and honor them. With long life will He satisfy them and show them His salvation, which includes not only eternal life with Him, but safety, preservation, deliverance from danger and apprehension, health, and well-being.

Your words are a life and death matter. They will ensnare you or they will deliver you.

Sharon:

First Peter 3:10 KJV says, **"For he that will love life, and see good days, let him refrain his tongue from evil, and his lips that they speak no guile."** *The New King James Version* of this verse says, **"He who would love life and see good days, let him refrain his tongue from evil, and his lips from speaking deceit."**

Peter is saying, "If we are going to love life and see good days, we have to refrain our tongue from speaking contrary to God's Word." Sometimes people will speak Scriptures, but their conversation is raunchy! We have to put a bit on our tongue, like James says.

Billy Joe:

We've been around some married couples who started talking divorce in a joking manner in their conversation with each other. We began to notice how people were walking in exactly what they were saying. They thought they were joking, but remember, the devil isn't joking. If he can get your tongue going the wrong direction, just like the bit in a horse's mouth, he will lead you in a wrong direction.

Some people say, "Those were just idle words." Wait a minute! Jesus said we would give account of every idle word. (See Matthew 12:36,37.) That means every word we speak has a harvest attached to it. The harvest from your words will either work for you or work against you, according to what you have been speaking.

If you want God's Word to work in your life, you must begin to believe that everything you say will come to pass. Faith is a combination force and it works out of your heart, out of your lips, with your actions, and with a renewed mind. If you are constantly joking, kidding, or speaking things that aren't true, the devil loves it because then when you speak God's Word, it won't work.

Jesus put it this way in Mark 11:23:

> **For assuredly, I say to you, whoever says to this mountain, "Be removed and be cast into the sea," and**

does not doubt in his heart, but believes that those things
he says will be done, he will have whatever he says.

We are to call things that are not as though they were,
just as Abraham did. (See Romans 4:17.) We are to speak
to the mountains in life to be removed, whatever they are.
If you want to be a joyful person, begin to say, *Lord, Your
joy is my strength. Thank You, Lord, for the fruit of joy in
my life. Thank You that You have given me joy that no man
can take from me. Thank You, Lord, that the redeemed of
the Lord have everlasting joy upon their heads.*

Many Christians are controlled by their feelings. They
feel good. They feel bad. They feel happy. They feel sad.
They're up and they're down. But when you become a Word
person, you don't base your life on how you feel. You base
your life on what God's Word says.

When someone asks, "How are you doing?" tell them,
"I am blessed." They may respond, "But look at these cir-
cumstances." You reply, "It doesn't matter, I am blessed.
God is able to turn things around in one moment."

The things that are around us don't have to control us.
The circumstances don't have to move us. We don't have
to be moved and we don't have to be shaken, because our
life is built on the rock of hearing and doing God's Word.

Sharon:

Acts 10:38 says:

How God anointed Jesus of Nazareth with the Holy Spirit and with power, who went about doing good and healing all who were oppressed by the devil, for God was with Him.

Billy Joe:

If someone asks you, "What's up?" you can say, *I am! I'm seated with Christ in heavenly places. The blessings of the Lord are chasing me and coming on me. God is perfecting everything that concerns me. He is making me a thousand times more in every area of my life and ministry – in joy, in blessing, in victory, in glory, in signs and wonders. I am strong in the Lord and in the power of His might.* (Ephesians 2:6, 6:10; Psalm 138:8; Deuteronomy 1:11, 28:8.)

Sharon:

We have an elderly lady in our church who moved to Tulsa after her husband passed away. She was bitten by a tick and the medical diagnosis was, "If you live, you will be in a wheelchair the rest of your life."

She began to hear and confess the Word of the Lord: *I shall not die but live and declare the works of the Lord. I am going from strength to strength, and I can do all things through Christ who strengthens me.* (Psalm 118:17; Philippians 4:13.)

This woman went from the wheelchair to a walker to walking in her own strength. Then she went through Victory World Missions Training Center, and she has been on the mission field several times in these last few years. Alice Bush kept speaking her faith and she overcame the physical challenges in her body.

Billy Joe:

It has been over ten years since that happened. She is in her late seventies and she is still active in missions work. She has been satisfied with the fruit of her mouth. You, like Alice, can change your circumstances by believing and speaking and acting upon the promises of God's Word.

4

An angel spoke to Daniel, "I have come because of your words."

Daniel 10:12

4

YOUR WORDS WILL DELIVER YOU
OR BIND YOU

Your words will put you over or they will put you under. We see this principle played out in Numbers, chapters 13 and 14, with the twelve spies Moses sent to spy out the promised land. Caleb and Joshua's words took them into the promised land, while the remaining ten spies' negative confession doomed them to the wilderness.

Let's pick up on the report of this occurrence in verses 26-33 of Numbers, chapter 13:

> **Now they departed and came back to Moses and Aaron and all the congregation of the children of Israel in the Wilderness of Paran, at Kadesh; they brought back word to them and to all the congregation, and showed them the fruit of the land.**
>
> **Then they told him, and said: "We went to the land where you sent us. It truly flows with milk and honey, and this is its fruit.**
>
> **Nevertheless the people who dwell in the land are strong; the cities are fortified and very large; moreover we saw the descendants of Anak there.**

The Amalekites dwell in the land of the South; the Hittites, the Jebusites, and the Amorites dwell in the mountains; and the Canaanites dwell by the sea and along the banks of the Jordan."

Then Caleb quieted the people before Moses, and said, "Let us go up at once and take possession, for we are well able to overcome it."

But the men who had gone up with him said, "We are not able to go up against the people, for they are stronger than we."

And they gave the children of Israel a bad report of the land which they had spied out, saying, "The land through which we have gone as spies is a land that devours its inhabitants, and all the people whom we saw in it are men of great stature.

There we saw giants (the descendants of Anak came from the giants); and we were like grasshoppers in our own sight, and so we were in their sight."

Are you a grasshopper? Is that how you see yourself? Let's continue with this same account in Numbers, chapter 14:

So all the congregation lifted up their voices and cried, and the people wept that night.

And all the children of Israel complained against Moses and Aaron, and the whole congregation said to them, "If only we had died in the land of Egypt! Or if only we had died in this wilderness!"

Verses 1,2

When we think of wilderness in America, we think of land that is full of brush and trees. But the wilderness in Judea was a barren, rocky desert. The Israelites said, **"If only we had died in this wilderness!"** (v. 2).

> **"Why has the Lord brought us to this land to fall by the sword, that our wives and children should become victims? Would it not be better for us to return to Egypt?"**
>
> **So they said to one another, "Let us select a leader and return to Egypt."**
>
> **Then Moses and Aaron fell on their faces before all the assembly of the congregation of the children of Israel.**
>
> **But Joshua the son of Nun and Caleb the son of Jephunneh, who were among those who had spied out the land, tore their clothes;**
>
> **And they spoke to all the congregation of the children of Israel, saying: "The land we passed through to spy out is an exceedingly good land.**
>
> **"If the Lord delights in us, then He will bring us into this land and give it to us, a land which flows with milk and honey.**
>
> **"Only do not rebel against the Lord, nor fear the people of the land, for they are our bread; their protection has departed from them, and the Lord is with us. Do not fear them."**
>
> **And all the congregations said to stone them with stones. Now the glory of the Lord appeared in the tabernacle of meeting before all the children of Israel.**
>
> **Verses 3-10**

51

When you read these verses from chapters 13 and 14 of Numbers, you go back and forth from a bad report to a good report, a good report to a bad report.

Joshua and Caleb stood up and told the Israelites what God told them:

> "Let us go up at once and take possession, for we are well able to overcome it . . .
>
> "The land we passed through to spy out is an exceedingly good land.
>
> "If the Lord delights in us, then He will bring us into this land and give it to us, 'a land which flows with milk and honey.'
>
> "Only do not rebel against the Lord, nor fear the people of the land, for they are our bread; their protection has departed from them, and the Lord is with us. Do not fear them."
>
> Numbers 13:30, 14:7-9

God said the land was **"a land which flows with milk and honey"** (v. 8). That means it's a land of blessing, of abundance, of prosperity. "Milk and honey" refer to every good thing.

God had said, "I'm going to give you cities you didn't build, fields you have not tilled, storehouses you did not fill." (See Deuteronomy 6:10,11.) The Israelites had experienced supernatural deliverance from the plagues, which included frogs, lice, flies, pestilence that killed all the livestock, hail, locusts, thick darkness for three days, and death to the firstborn of the Egyptians.

Although it had only been a short time since the Israelites experienced the supernatural deliverance of God, they forgot what God had done for them. When they faced new giants and new problems, they went back into the realm of fear and their words testified to it. But right in the middle of it, Joshua and Caleb said, "We are well able. Let's go up at once and take it. If God is for us, and He has already told us He is, then we will be able to take this land."

God spoke to Moses:

"How long will these people reject Me? And how long will they not believe Me, with all the signs which I have performed among them?

"I will strike them with the pestilence and disinherit them, and I will make of you a nation greater and mightier than they."

Numbers 14:11,12

Moses interceded for the Israelites: **"Pardon the iniquity of this people, I pray, according to the greatness of Your mercy, just as You have forgiven this people, from Egypt even until now"** (Numbers 14:19).

The Lord accepted Moses' intercession for the Israelites, saying:

"I have pardoned, according to your word; but truly, as I live, all the earth shall be filled with the glory of the Lord –

"Because all these men who have seen My glory and the signs which I did in Egypt and in the wilderness, and have put Me to the test now these ten times, and have not heeded My voice, they certainly shall not see the land of which I swore to their fathers, nor shall any of those who rejected Me see it.

"But My servant Caleb, because he has a different spirit in him and has followed Me fully, I will bring into the land where he went, and his descendants shall inherit it."

Verses 20-24

God wasn't real excited about the attitude of the Israelites. He assured Moses that the people hadn't rejected him, but "they have rejected Me and My word."

In verse 28 of Numbers 14, God said, **"'As I live,' says the Lord, 'just as you have spoken in My hearing, so I will do to you.'"** In other words, "I am going to do to you exactly what you have spoken to Me."

Then God goes on:

"The carcasses of you who have complained against Me shall fall in this wilderness, all of you who were numbered, according to your entire number, from twenty years old and above.

"Except for Caleb the son of Jephunneh and Joshua

the son of Nun, you shall by no means enter the land which I swore I would make you dwell in."

Numbers 14:29,30

God held those twenty years old and upward accountable for their words. They had said, "If only we had died in the land of Egypt! Or if only we had died in this wilderness!" (Numbers 14:2). God said, "You've got it!" Joshua and Caleb said, "We are well able to go in and possess the land." God said, "You've got it!" This is why your words are so important. Either they will deliver you or they will bind you.

5

"I tell you the truth, if anyone says to this mountain, 'Go, throw yourself into the sea,' and does not doubt in his heart but believes that what he says will happen, it will be done for him. Therefore I tell you, whatever you ask for in prayer, believe that you have received it, and it will be yours."

Mark 11:23,24 NIV

5

THERE'S CREATIVE POWER IN THE SPOKEN WORD

In the beginning, God gave man dominion. (Genesis 1:26-28.) That word "dominion" means authority and power. God's authority was released through the words He spoke. When He spoke, things happened. Genesis, chapter 1, is filled with creation manifestations, all of which came in response to God's words.

God delegated His authority and dominion in the earth to man, and that authority and dominion are activated with words. Satan came to steal that authority and tempted Adam and Eve to disobey God and sin, and they did. They were driven from the garden, yet man was still made in the image and likeness of God. Man still had a degree of dominion and authority as a human being, but the good news is, the second Adam, Jesus Christ, returned, paid for our sin, was raised from the dead, and restored the dominion and authority to us that Adam lost.

Romans 5:17 says:

> **For if by one man's offense death reigned through the one, much more those who receive abundance of grace**

and the gift of righteousness will reign in life through the One, Jesus Christ.

God's Word has creative power, so when man was made in His image and likeness, we were made to have that same authority, dominion, and power to be released in our words. The power of choice is in our words, and the dominion and authority of God are exercised through our words.

Hebrews 11:3 says that God created the worlds with His words:

By faith we understand that the worlds were framed by the word of God, so that the things which are seen were not made of things which are visible.

In Numbers, chapters 13 and 14, we saw life and we saw death as a result of the words that were spoken. Life to Joshua and Caleb whose words were in agreement with God; death to the other ten spies whose words were in agreement with Satan.

Psalm 119:130 says, **"The entrance of Your words give light...."** If we hide God's Word in our hearts, we will be kept from sin. When we put the Word of God in our heart in abundance, we are going to speak that Word with authority and power.

Your words are either speaking life or they are speaking death, and you will reap a harvest from them. Words are seeds and when they are planted, they will come up.

When you plant the incorruptible seed of God's Word (1 Peter 1:23), you're going to reap a harvest of God's righteousness. Speak negative, defeating, discouraging, fear-filled words and that type of harvest will come up in your life.

Your Words Can Turn the Course of Your Life

Your life is following your words! When people begin to understand the power released through their own words – for good or for evil – many have said, "If only I had known long ago." The good news is, you can change the course of your life today!

Jesus Christ bought you with His blood. The heavenly Father has said that you are a new creation in Christ Jesus, His Son. He says, "I put My hand upon you and everything your hand touches is blessed. You are valuable to Me." Begin to say what God says about you. Agree with God's Word.

Salvation is tied to the words of our mouth:

"The word is near you, in your mouth and in your heart" (that is, the word of faith which we preach):

"That if you confess with your mouth the Lord Jesus and believe in your heart that God has raised Him from the dead, you will be saved.

> **"For with the heart one believes unto righteousness,
> and with the mouth confession is made unto salvation."**
>
> **Romans 10:8-10**

If you really believe something in your heart, you will say it with your mouth. And if you will continue to say what God says long enough, it will get down in your heart until you believe it.

Psalm 23:1 says, **"The Lord is my shepherd."** Begin to speak it: *The Lord is my Shepherd.* If you say it long enough, you will begin to believe that the Lord is your Shepherd. It's true whether you believe it and speak it or not. But if you will begin to say it because it is truth, it will go down in your heart and it will change your thinking. This is how your mind is renewed. This same principle applies to all of the promises of God's Word.

Christianity Is "The Great Confession"

Confession is the essence of Christianity. In fact, Christianity is often called "the great confession."

Hebrews 10:23 KJV says, **"Let us hold fast the profession of our faith without wavering; (for he is faithful that promised)."** Jesus is the High Priest over the profession of our faith.

After Daniel's twenty-one days of praying, an angel

came to him and said, **"I have come because of your words"** (Daniel 10:12).

I'm telling you, the angels are coming for your words. If you are speaking fear, doubt, disaster, calamity, and unbelief, they will simply fold their wings! But if you'll declare the Word of God with faith, the angels will hearken to your words.

Psalm 103:20 confirms this truth: **"Bless the Lord, you His angels, who excel in strength, who do His word, heeding the voice of His word."**

Proverbs 13:2 KJV says, **"A man shall eat good by the fruit of his mouth. . . ."** Some people have a negative connotation of eating their words. Eating your words is an irrevocable law, the same as gravity.

The words that you are speaking will affect the future of your children, the blessing of your marriage, the health in your body, your performance on your job, and the directions that you take.

Bow the knee of your confession only to Jesus. Do not bow to your own words, to the circumstances, to the opinions of others, to what's going on in the world, or to what the devil says. Refuse to speak things that are not truth according to God's Word, which is the *final authority.*

6

*"Some people are tripped by their lip
and hung by their tongue!"*

Billy Joe Daugherty

6

MIXING FAITH WITH YOUR WORDS

Therefore, since a promise remains of entering His rest, let us fear lest any of you seem to have come short of it.

For indeed the gospel was preached to us as well as to them; but the word which they heard did not profit them, not being mixed with faith in those who heard it.

Hebrews 4:1,2

The promises of God will not produce results or profit you unless you mix faith with them – *believing, speaking,* and *acting* upon God's Word. (See 2 Corinthians 4:13.) Just as a child imitates his father, we are to pattern our faith after the faith of God.

Where do we get the pattern for love? From God because He is love. The pattern for joy? From the joy of the Lord. The faith of God? From God.

Jesus was walking from Bethany over the Mount of Olives, down the Kidron Valley, up into Jerusalem with His twelve disciples right before He was crucified. He saw a fig tree that should have had figs on it. But it only had leaves, for Scripture says, **"It was not the season of figs"** (Mark 11:13).

Jesus pointed to the fig tree and said, **"Let no one eat fruit from you ever again"** (Mark 11:14). He kept right on walking, went into the temple, and cast out the people who were buying and selling, perverting His house from being a house of prayer.

The following day Jesus and His disciples passed by the fig tree He had cursed and it was dried up from the roots. Peter said, **"Rabbi, look! The fig tree which You cursed has withered away"** (v. 21). Jesus said to Peter and the other disciples:

> **"Have faith in God. For assuredly, I say to you, whoever says to this mountain, 'Be removed and be cast into the sea,' and does not doubt in his heart, but believes that those things he says will be done, he will have whatever he says.**
>
> **"Therefore I say to you, whatever things you ask when you pray, believe that you receive them, and you will have them."**
>
> **Mark 11:22-24**

Faith Calls Things That Are Not As Though They Are

You will have what you say when you believe that what you say will come to pass. Jesus demonstrated faith, then He said, "Have the God-kind of faith." The faith He is talking about is the kind where God called things that were not as though they were. (See Romans 4:17.)

God called Abraham "the father of nations" before Abraham ever had a child. Abraham was nearly a hundred years old and Sarah was ninety. Abraham began saying, "Don't call me Abram anymore. I'm Abraham, the father of nations." He was calling things that were not as though they were.

Some people have called themselves poor for so long that it is deeply entrenched in their belief system. Or they have called themselves sick. Begin to say, *I am the blessed of the Lord. I am the healed of the Lord. I am redeemed. I am the head and not the tail, above only and not beneath.*

What God says is truth. Sometimes people say, "Come on, tell the truth. How are you really doing?" Is what the doctor says "truth"? Is what the newspaper says "truth"? No way! It doesn't matter what people say or what the circumstances look like. Those things are all temporal, which means subject to change!

Second Corinthians 4:18 says, **"We do not look at the things which are seen, but at the things which are not seen. For the things which are seen are temporary, but the things which are not seen are eternal."**

If you base your life on the things you say that are not in agreement with God's Word, it's like basing your life on the weather. It's going to change from day to day. We do not look at things which are seen, but at things which are unseen, for the things that are seen are temporary, but the things which are unseen are eternal. The doctor's report is subject to change, but God's Word will never change. The Dow Jones Average changes continually, but God's Word never changes.

Are you going to believe in things that you can see more than in the things that are unseen? Will you trust in the temporal or the eternal? Many times women go the beauty shop to get what's called a "permanent." All of us men know it's not a permanent! It's a temporary!

When someone asks you, "How are you feeling?" you can answer with the truth: *Jesus bore my sicknesses and He carried my diseases. With His stripes I am healed.*

Whether they realize it or not, most people have been telling things that aren't truth. They may have been factual according to what was visible, but truth is eternal and unchanging. It is always the same. The important thing is that we *believe* and *speak* what God says. The spirit of faith is *believing* and *speaking* what God says. It started with God, then Noah, Abraham, and David when he faced Goliath the giant, then Daniel. Hebrews, chapter 11, gives us a list of people who *believed* and *spoke* God's Word in the face of trials and difficulties.

The Bible says we have the same spirit of faith. Now, you may not be called to do what David did or what Noah did in building an ark, but God has called you to do something. It's important that you exercise the spirit of faith. It may be in getting your tuition money for school; the provision for your family to have food, shelter, and transportation; getting the money you need to be prepared for ministry and/or the mission field. It's important that you *believe* and *speak* the Word of God.

An Example of Faith in Action

Luke, chapter 1, verses 26-38 give us a powerful demonstration of the spirit of faith in the life of Mary. Let's look at "faith in action" in this account:

Now in the sixth month the angel Gabriel was sent by God to a city of Galilee named Nazareth,

To a virgin betrothed to a man whose name was Joseph, of the house of David. The virgin's name was Mary.

And having come in, the angel said to her, "Rejoice, highly favored one, the Lord is with you; blessed are you among women!"

But when she saw him, she was troubled at his saying, and considered what manner of greeting this was.

Then the angel said to her, "Do not be afraid, Mary, for you have found favor with God.

"And behold, you will conceive in your womb and bring forth a Son, and shall call His name JESUS.

"He will be great, and will be called the Son of the Highest; and the Lord God will give Him the throne of His father David.

"And He will reign over the house of Jacob forever, and of His kingdom there will be no end."

Then Mary said to the angel, "How can this be, since I do not know a man?"

And the angel answered and said to her, "The Holy Spirit will come upon you, and the power of the Highest will overshadow you; therefore, also, that Holy One who is to be born will be called the Son of God.

"Now indeed, Elizabeth your relative has also conceived a son in her old age; and this is now the sixth month for her who was called barren.

"For with God nothing will be impossible."

Then Mary said, "Behold the maidservant of the Lord! Let it be to me according to your word." And the angel departed from her.

The angel came to Mary with the Word of God, and Mary said, "How can this be?" So in the natural, she did not understand. How can it be that you could walk in victory? How can it be that you could walk in health? How can it be that all of your children could be saved, filled with the Holy Ghost, and serving God? How can it be that you would be out of debt and prospering in every area of your life? How can it be that you would preach Christ to the nations of the earth? How can it be?

When Mary asked the angel, **"How can this be, since I do not know a man?"** (Luke 1:34), the angel said, **"The Holy Spirit will come upon you . . ."** (v. 35).

What happens when you start speaking God's Word? The Holy Spirit comes upon you and performs that Word. He brings it to pass. He causes that Word to become flesh and to be fulfilled.

How do you take a seed – a promise from God's Word – and see it become a harvest? The Word of God is called the incorruptible seed of God's Word. How do you take that inside of you? How did Mary start with a tiny seed inside of her and it became the Son of God? How did the seed of the Word become flesh? If you get a revelation of this, you will see that what happened to Mary happens every time you believe the Word of God. You are giving birth to a part of the life of Christ in the earth.

Mary was the only one who could give birth to Jesus naturally so He could come and redeem the earth. Every time you believe for the joy of the Lord and you begin to confess it, joy will grow inside of you, it will come out of you, and people will behold Jesus in His joy in you.

This same principle is true for peace. As you confess the promise of John 14:27, peace is conceived inside of you and it begins to grow. **"Peace I leave with you, My peace I give to you; not as the world gives do I give to you. Let not your heart be troubled, neither let it be afraid."**

As you *believe* and *speak* the Word, it is planted in the womb of your faith. Just as development takes place in a natural womb, in the womb of your spirit you are nurturing peace and joy, victory and healing.

Hold fast to the promises you are believing and confessing. Don't give up. The promises are growing inside of you. Sometimes people abort their promises through unbelief.

There can be unbelieving believers and unbelieving family members whose words "stab you in your heart" and your dream dies. You have to hold on to that word, protect it, guard it, and say, "I am going to see this thing come full term."

The moment Mary said to the angel, **"Let it be to me according to your word"** (Luke 1:38), her miracle was on!

You can go around speaking disaster, calamity, tragedy, lack and poverty, and sickness, and saying, "No one in our family has ever amounted to anything." Either you'll dig a rut with the words of your own mouth or you will get a revelation of God's Word and begin to say, *I'm in a new family. I've got a new bloodline. My Father loves me and cares for me. Jesus Christ has redeemed me by His blood, and I have been translated into the Kingdom of Light. I am the head and not the tail, above only and not beneath. I am a new creation. All of those old things have passed away. I'm a child of God, an heir of God, and a joint heir with Jesus Christ.*

You will rise or fall to the level of your confession. You can turn the course of your whole ship by getting a hold of the words of your mouth.

In John 6:28, the disciples asked Jesus, **"What shall we do, that we may work the works of God?"** Jesus said, **"This is the work of God, that you believe in Him whom He sent"** (v. 29). Our job is to believe the promises of God, and God will perform those promises in our life.

What You Confess You Will Possess

Sharon and I called peace and harmony into our marriage. Many couples call strife and divorce into their marriage by joking and speaking them into existence. Fear and death are part of many people's words.

Charles Capps, a farmer from England, Arkansas, began to get a hold on the importance of the words of our lips. He had some fields that weren't producing and God told him to speak over those fields, "You will produce."

His crops began to yield a greater harvest than his neighbors. Why? Because of the power he released through his words.

Begin to speak over your children: *My children are taught by the Lord and they are obedient to His will. Great is their peace and undisturbed composure* (Isaiah 54:13 AMP).

Begin to say: *In my path is life and there is no death. This will be the best day of my life.* Some folks get up and say, "Oh, my, it's Monday." When you run into them, it's like Mr. Gloom or Miss Doom walked in. You can be different as you begin to decree and declare what will come your way.

For too long people have limited this truth to being born again. But this principle works with every promise in God's Word that you believe with your heart and speak with your mouth. The Word is near you, in your mouth to speak and in your heart to believe.

What you confess you will possess. It's like calling the dog. In our case we say, "Here Freckles. Here Daisy." They come wagging their tails. Daisy knocks everything around and even knocks Freckles over. She is a big dog and funny as can be. She talks, but the funniest thing is those who talk back to her!

When you go out in the yard and say, "Here dog," and

the dog is not there, you are calling things that are not as though they were! If most of us had been God when there was nothing but darkness and blackness in the universe, instead of saying, "Let there be light," we would have looked out and said, "Wow, it's dark out there!" We've got to change our thinking. *We need to call things as God says they are.*

You need to start calling your prosperity home, your healing home, your sons and daughters home. How about joy and victory? Why not live in total joy? The Bible says everlasting joy will be upon your head. Jesus says, "The joy I give you, no man can take from you." Joy is one of the fruit of the Spirit listed in Galatians, chapter 5. You take it by *believing* it in your heart and *declaring* it with your mouth. Start saying, *The joy of the Lord is my strength. I cast my cares on the Lord.* Get rid of bitterness and resentment and unforgiveness, and become a doer of the Word.

Years ago when Rhema Bible Training Center first started, Sharon and I were youth directors in the church where it began so we got in on it. We became acquainted with an older couple who also attended Rhema that year. Two of their four children moved to Tulsa from Florida with them, but two older children did not. The older son lived on the beaches of Florida. He was into alcohol, drugs, and immorality.

When his parents moved to Tulsa to attend Rhema, Greg didn't have anyone to wash his clothes and there was no more home cooking, so he finally decided to come to Oklahoma. He called his parents and asked if he could come and stay with them. He was about nineteen years old at the time. They said, "Yes, but you will have to go to church and to youth meetings."

Greg would come to church and youth group, but he would cut up, make fun, and cause trouble. You could smell alcohol or tobacco on his breath many times.

His mother and father had gotten a hold of what I'm talking about – the power of your words. They read Acts 16:31: **"Believe on the Lord Jesus Christ, and you will be saved, you and your household."** They prayed Mark 11:24: **"Whatever things you ask when you pray, believe that you receive them, and you will have them."** They started thanking God that all of their children were saved, baptized with the Holy Spirit, and serving the Lord.

Every time Sharon and I saw Greg's mother, she would say, "Isn't Greg doing wonderful?" We wanted to ask, "Are you talking about the one who comes to our youth group?" Sharon and I were just learning about believing and confessing God's Word at this point in our lives. We just thought Greg's mom was "out of it"! She wasn't moved by what she saw, what she felt, or what she smelled. She just kept confessing God's Word.

Hebrews 10:23 KJV says, **"Let us hold fast the profession** [or confession] **of our faith without wavering; (for he is faithful that promised)."**

So how long should we confess what God says? How about *forever?* How long will the Word of God be true? *Forever!* This isn't something we try for three days to see if it will work. Many people have jumped out of the boat on this because they thought it was a gimmick to try to get something.

In Matthew 4:4 Jesus said, **"Man shall not live by bread alone, but by every word that proceeds from the mouth of God."** Sharon and I decided we would walk by faith and live by the Word of God.

We had a youth party at our house one night after church service. Greg knew there would be food and girls so he came. He sat by the door where he could exit quickly if something started to happen. We were having a little afterglow and he had a six-pack in his car for a later afterglow! We were eating and everyone was talking. Kids were all over the room.

Suddenly a young man, who was sitting next to Greg, raised his hand and asked for prayer, so all of the kids descended on him. Greg kept right on eating. I was standing in front of the young man who asked for prayer. The Lord said, "Lay your hand on Greg's knee and pray for him." I reached over and said, "In the name of Jesus," and the power of God shot through him like electricity. He dropped his plate and began to worship and praise God with tears streaming down his face. He confessed Jesus as his Savior, he was baptized with the Holy Spirit, and called into the ministry that evening. From there he went to Bible school and became a youth pastor.

"Your words will bury you or they will resurrect you. They will take you over the top or put you under. The topic of your words in the Bible isn't a side issue. It's at the very core of the Word of God!"

Billy Joe Daugherty

7

YOUR CONFESSION WILL BRING POSSESSION

Have you ever been stabbed with words? Have someone's words pierced you like a sword? Have you ever been tripped by your lip or hung by your tongue? Have you ever put your foot in your mouth?

Right now you are living in the words that you have spoken in days gone by. You are reaping the harvest of the seeds of your words that you have released out of your lips. Galatians 6:7 says, **"Whatever a man sows, that he will also reap."**

Second Corinthians 9:6-11 has something to say about sowing and reaping:

> **But this I say: He who sows sparingly will also reap sparingly, and he who sows bountifully will also reap bountifully.**
>
> **So let each one give as he purposes in his heart, not grudgingly or of necessity; for God loves a cheerful giver.**
>
> **And God is able to make all grace abound toward**

you, that you, always having all sufficiency in all things, may have an abundance for every good work.

As it is written: "He has dispersed abroad, He has given to the poor; His righteousness endures forever."

Now may He who supplies seed to the sower, and bread for food, supply and multiply the seed you have sown and increase the fruits of your righteousness,

While you are enriched in everything for all liberality, which causes thanksgiving through us to God.

We tend to look at these verses only in terms of finances. But what you sow in the realm of the spirit will also come back to you in multiplied form. If you sow right words, you will eat good by the fruit of your mouth. (Proverbs 18:20,21.)

Proverbs 6:2 says, **"You are snared by the words of your mouth...."** You are taken captive by your own words. You are snared or liberated by the words that you speak. Your words will turn loose the blessings of God, or they will turn loose the curse of the enemy. That's why the devil has sown many phrases of fear and death into the human language.

People talk about them being "scared to death," "dying to get there," "dead sure," "afraid so." If the devil can get people to speak the law of sin and death and fear and death, then sin and death and fear and death will work inside of their life.

Jesus Christ has set us free from the law of sin and death by the law of the Spirit of life that is in Him. We are called to speak words of life, which are words that will agree with God's Word.

Matthew 12:35 says, **"A good man out of the good treasure of his heart brings forth good things, and an evil man out of the evil treasure brings forth evil things."** In other words, your mouth draws on what is in your heart.

The words of your mouth will cause you to possess the promised land like Joshua and Caleb, or it will cause you to die in the wilderness like the rest of the Israelites twenty years old and upward. Your words will bury you or resurrect you. Your words will take you down or put you over the top. Faith-filled words can change your life. Your mouth has awesome power.

What would happen if you began to speak faith-filled words every day, such as: *I am more than a conqueror through Jesus Christ. Greater is He who is in me than he who is in the world. The Lord is my Shepherd, I shall not lack or have want of anything. My cup runs over. Jesus came that I might have life and have it more abundantly. This is my day of abundant life. This is the day the Lord has made, and I'm going to rejoice and be glad in it. The joy of the Lord is my strength. Thank You, Lord, that Your mercies endure forever, and they are new to me every morning.*

Redirecting Your Life with the Rudder of Your Tongue!

You can redirect your life with the words that you speak. The New Testament clearly explains this in the book of James, as we discussed earlier. James says that your tongue is like the bit in a horse's mouth. Whichever way you pull on the reins connected to that two and a half inch bit, the whole horse will go.

James also said that your tongue is like the rudder or the controls on a ship. Whichever way the captain turns those controls and maneuvers that rudder, the massive ship will turn. Even so is your tongue! Whichever way your tongue goes is the way your life will go.

If you feel like you're sailing into troubled waters, why not turn your ship around by beginning to declare: *I am the blessed of the Lord. I am the healed of the Lord. I am the delivered of the Lord. God is my peace, He is my victory, and He is my light and my salvation.*

Jesus Whipped the Devil with Words

In Matthew 4:1-11 the devil tempted Jesus three times and Jesus overcame the temptations with, "It is written," then quoting an appropriate Word promise. If the devil came at Jesus three times, how many times do you think he's going to come at you? If Jesus overcame the devil by the words of His mouth, what do you think you are going to have to do to overcome the devil?

The Bible says Jesus took upon Himself human flesh and was made in the likeness of man so He could leave us an example that we could follow. Jesus was tempted in every point just like we are, and He took the Word that is available to every believer and defeated the devil!

You see, if Jesus had something that you and I do not have, then He would not be an example that we could follow. He taught us by the way He lived that we could live the same way. One of the reasons people are unable to live like Jesus is they don't study His example with the purpose of following it. They read the stories and think, *Oh, wasn't that wonderful! He was awesome!* They don't understand that He lived that way, walked that way, and did those things to show us how to live an overcoming, abundant life.

In Sunday school or in Vacation Bible School when we were little kids, we were taught, "Be like Jesus." But somehow when people get to be adults, they say, "You can't be like Jesus." What happened between the time they were in Vacation Bible School and the time they grew up? It's called doubt, unbelief, and suspicion of God's Word. We are called to be like Jesus, regardless of our age. And if He had to speak the Word to resist the devil, so do we. *The devil is not going to flee from your life until you start speaking the Word of God.*

Notice, Jesus didn't quote the author of the verses. He didn't say, "And Moses said." Or, "In verse so-and-so." He did not give a geographical background or say who the local king was at the time.

If you are going to speak the Word of God with authority, you are going to have to believe that God's Word is true, that it has authority and power, and that you can take it right out of the Bible and quote it as real.

Jesus wrote the book! He didn't explain what came before the verse and He didn't explain what came after it. He just took the sword and went wham! When you have faith in God's Word, it will have the same power against the devil as it had against the devil in Jesus' days on earth. You have to move from doubt, unbelief, and suspicion about God's Word to the fact that you believe God's Word has integrity. God said what He meant and He meant what He said. You can take any promise from the Bible and speak it in faith.

Using the Sword of the Word

Have you been praying, "Oh, Lord, get the devil off of me"? God gave you a weapon against the devil and that is His Word. If you don't use the sword of the Word, the devil isn't going to budge. The sword of the Spirit, which is the Word of God, is the only piece of armor that is specifically identified as an offensive weapon, but it also operates as a defensive weapon.

I'm talking about how to defeat the Monday morning blues. I'm talking about how to defeat strife in your home – arguing and fighting among family members. I'm talking about how to whip sickness and disease. This is real stuff! How are you going to overcome fear if you live in a neighborhood that's having some troubles? What are you going to do at 4:00 in the morning when you hear that rattling out behind the house? What are you going to do when you see the Dow Jones Averages go up and down? What are you going to do when a high government official reveals his perverse lifestyle? What are you going to do when you read the paper which tells of bombs that have gone off in different parts of the world? Either you are going to speak fear or faith, and your words will take you over or put you under. They will cause life or death to come to you.

The psalmist David said, **"Let the words of my mouth and the meditation of my heart be acceptable in Your sight, O Lord, my strength and my Redeemer"** (Psalm 19:14). He also said in Psalm 141:3, **"Set a guard, O Lord, over my mouth; keep watch over the door of my lips."**

If you are going to speak faith, one of the things you

89

are going to have to do is start watching your words. Faith-filled words will come from a heart that is determined to speak them. It's not an accidental exercise!

Sometimes people say, "We just say that in jest. We don't really mean it." Well, how does your heart know when you mean something? If every day all day long you are speaking things that you don't really mean, then when you get ready to talk to cancer and tell it to get out of your body, or out of your son or your daughter, your wife or your mother's body, there is no faith in you. You have robbed yourself of faith by continually speaking things that are in jest, doubt, and unbelief.

I'm talking about a *lifestyle principle* that will bury you or resurrect you, take you over the top or put you under. This isn't some side issue in the Bible. This is at the very heart of it.

Everything God created, He did it with words. You are made in His likeness and image. He planned for us to create our world with faith-filled words, following His example. I'm not talking about another Saturn, Uranus, or Pluto. I'm talking about where we live! You can change your world from a place of chaos, confusion, sickness, defeat, sin, and failure into a place of light, victory, holiness, righteousness, and truth. You will do it with the words of your mouth.

If you haven't been guarding your tongue, this is not a word to condemn you. It is a word to help you turn your ship around. These things are all in the Bible. Proverbs is filled with the revelation of how powerful our tongue is, but until we get in the Word, we will perish for lack of knowledge. (Hosea 4:6.)

Put on Your Armor!

God has a good plan for your life, but the other side of the coin is, the devil also has a plan for your life and it's not good. You've got to have on the whole armor of God to withstand Satan's plans.

Is your life on the rock or on the sand? The floods, the winds, the storms of life come against both houses, but for those whose foundation is on the bedrock of God's Word, they will stand while the storms rage. They will still be standing – waving and shouting the victory – when the storm passes. If you are anchored on the foundation of God's Word, the devil's plans won't affect you. Hallelujah!

In Ephesians, chapter 6, Paul lists the armor of God:

Finally, my brethren, be strong in the Lord and in the power of His might.

Put on the whole armor of God, that you may be able to stand against the wiles of the devil,

> **For we do not wrestle against flesh and blood, but against principalities, against powers, against the rulers of the darkness of this age, against spiritual hosts of wickedness in the heavenly places.**
>
> **Verses 10-12**

This is talking about the demonic hierarchy. In the military, there are generals, captains, lieutenants, on down the line. In the Navy you have admirals and again, right on down the line, second lieutenants, seamen first class and so forth. Paul is describing principalities, powers, and rulers of darkness in the heavenly places, so the devil has demonic spirits that operate in different places.

> **Therefore take up the whole armor of God, that you may be able to withstand in the evil day, and having done all, to stand.**
>
> **Verse 13**

You can withstand the devil's assaults by believing and speaking the promises of God.

> **Stand therefore, having girded your waist with truth, having put on the breastplate of righteousness,**
>
> **And having shod your feet with the preparation of the gospel of peace;**
>
> **Above all, taking the shield of faith with which you will be able to quench all the fiery darts of the wicked one.**
>
> **Verses 14-16**

The shield of faith is raised with what you *believe* and *speak.* You cannot raise your shield of faith without talking, and if you feel like you've got fiery darts stuck in your back and in your front and in your sides, it could be because the shield is on the floor! Maybe it's in the closet or even up in the attic! The shield of faith is lifted up with the words of your mouth: *In the name of Jesus, I am the righteousness of God in Christ, and no weapon formed against me will prosper. I have planted my seed and the devil is rebuked.* That is how you use your shield of faith.

If you don't have the shield of faith on, you are just playing religious games. We're in a war right now. It is not business as usual. This is why marriages, homes, families, bodies, and minds are being ripped off. It's time to take back what the devil has stolen.

> **And take the helmet of salvation, and the sword of the Spirit, which is the word of God;**
>
> **Praying always with all prayer and supplication in the Spirit, being watchful to this end with all perseverance and supplication for all the saints.**
>
> **Verses 17,18**

Hebrews 4:12 says, **"The word of God is living and powerful, and sharper than any two-edged sword, piercing even to the division of soul and spirit, and of joints and marrow, and is a discerner of the thoughts and intents of the heart."**

The Word can divide right down to the core of your being what you are thinking and what you are believing, what is of God, what is of the flesh, and what is of the devil. Some people hardly know the difference between day and night! But God's Word can divide and let you know when people are speaking truth and when they aren't speaking truth.

"The word of God is . . . sharper than any two-edged sword. . . ." The two-edged sword was an invention that the Romans capitalized on. It was a two and a half foot sword, sharpened on both sides with a point at the front. Whichever way a Roman soldier swung the sword, he was striking death.

Today it's very hard for people to comprehend a two-edged sword, so let me give you a modern-day example. When the United States dropped an atomic bomb on Hiroshima and then Nagasaki, the war was over. It was settled. There was no weapon to contend with the atomic bomb.

When the double-edged sword was invented, Rome conquered the whole world. No one could stop that weapon because no one had weapons like it.

The good news for Christians is, you've got a weapon that is more awesome than nuclear power. This weapon can destroy the strongholds of Satan. It can get into the realm of the atmosphere above us and dethrone evil prin-cipalities and powers over nations. The Word of God has awesome power.

The two Greek words for the Word of God are *logos* and *rhema*. *Logos* means the written Word, and *rhema* means the spoken Word. The "sword of the Spirit" in Ephesians 6:17 is talking about the spoken Word of God.

Until God's Word is released from your mouth, you're not going to defeat the devil. You can hold your Bible up and wave it, but that won't bother the devil. You can have one of those big fourteen-pounders sitting on your coffee table with ten years of dust on it! That is not going to defeat the devil. The Bible on a shelf or the Scripture verses you read ten years ago aren't going to defeat the devil. *It's the Word of God on your lips that will drive the devil out!*

Psalm 107:2 says, **"Let the redeemed of the Lord say so. . . ."** It's time to start saying what God says. That's what Jesus did. He said what God said. God's Word is true and it is forever settled in heaven. (Psalm 119:89.) The Word, which is true and eternal, will change that which is untrue and temporal.

The circumstances and situations in your life, as well as your feelings, are temporary. They are subject to change. Most people have lived their whole life by speaking about their temporary conditions and situations as if they were final truth. Maybe someone labeled them a nerd, a good-for-nothing, a loser, a wimp, and they've lived their whole life in the framework of those words. Then suddenly they get a revelation! *I am precious and valuable in God's sight. In Him I am more than a conqueror over any situation or obstacle. Greater is He who is in me than he who is in the world.*

You've got a choice. Are you going to believe what someone says about you, or are you going to believe what God says about you?

People who have lived their entire life bound with feelings of inferiority and inadequacy can be liberated once they hear, believe, speak, and act upon God's Word. The shield of faith will stop every fiery dart of the wicked one. The sword of the Spirit will drive the devil out.

The devil tried to get Jesus to presume upon the grace of God. When you are confessing God's Word, that doesn't mean you can do stupid things like jumping off the top of a building and saying, "God will give His angels charge over me." That's what the devil wanted Jesus to do, but Jesus saw through it. God's Word will work, but it doesn't mean you can grab a rattlesnake or take a loaded pistol, put it to to your head, and spin the revolver. Don't presume upon the grace of God by doing foolish things.

Confession of Psalm 23

Psalm 23 is one of the greatest confessions in the entire Bible. If you had no other confession to make, the confession of this psalm will turn the course of your ship:

The Lord is my shepherd; I shall not want.

He makes me to lie down in green pastures; He leads me beside the still waters.

He restores my soul; He leads me in the paths of righteousness for His name's sake.

Yea, though I walk through the valley of the shadow of death, I will fear no evil; for You are with me; Your rod and Your staff, they comfort me.

You prepare a table before me in the presence of my enemies; You anoint my head with oil; My cup runs over.

Surely goodness and mercy shall follow me all the days of my life; and I will dwell in the house of the Lord forever.

97

"What you say is coming your way. The words you sow are going to grow. What you speak you release. The angels are coming in response to God's Word that is spoken from your mouth."

Billy Joe Daugherty

8

FRAMING YOUR WORLD WITH GOD'S WORD

By faith we understand that the worlds were framed by the word of God, so that the things which are seen were not made of things which are visible.

Hebrews 11:3

This verse says it was through faith that the worlds were framed, or created, and brought into existence. They were created by the words of God's mouth. When He spoke, power was released to bring what He spoke into existence.

Your faith, though it is unseen, can bring things into the visible realm of your life. Your faith is in your heart and it is released through your words. So your faith, like God's, can bring the unseen into the visible realm.

God called things that were not as though they were. What do you want in your life? Start calling it in. What do you desire? What is God saying to you? It's time to speak it out.

Now think of a painter. He or she takes a brush and begins to paint a beautiful picture on a canvas. A framer puts a frame around it. What was only in the mind or in the heart of the artist and a framer is now a beautiful picture hanging on a wall.

So it is with God. He looked at darkness and chaos and He spoke and framed exactly what was in His heart. We have a beautiful earth with green grass, blue skies, oceans, rivers, mountains, and streams. It was in God's heart first, then He spoke it into existence.

You Can Frame Your World

Now, here's the important thing for you to grasp. You can frame your world – your marriage and family – with the Word of God in the same way God framed His world – with the words of His mouth. There is no need for you to create another Saturn, Uranus, Neptune, Pluto, or Jupiter, but there are some little orbits, some little planets, circling around your life called your mind, your job, your studies, and your body. Your little world can be painted and framed and created in the way that God wants it to be. It is done through the power of faith – the Word of God that is *believed* in your heart and *spoken* through your lips.

If there is something in your life that is not right and you want to change it, how are you going to do it? If your life looks dark, void, empty, and chaotic, how will you make it a beautiful picture? If your little universe, your home, your family, is nothing but a swirl of turmoil and strife, you never can pay your bills, there is constant sickness and disease, you can change it.

How would you like to have a world where your bills are all paid, your family is walking in health, you have peace and harmony in your home, and it is filled with the glory of God? You can frame your world and change it through the Word of God – *believing it in your heart, speaking it with your mouth, and becoming a doer of His Word.*

Jesus – Our Example of How To Frame Our World

In Mark, chapter 11, Jesus demonstrated His faith when He cursed the fig tree. Then He turned to His disciples and said:

Have faith in God. [You have faith in God.]

For assuredly, I say to you, whoever says to this mountain, "Be removed and be cast into the sea," and does not doubt in his heart, but believes that those things he says will be done, he will have whatever he says.

Therefore I say to you, whatever things you ask when you pray, believe that you receive them, and you will have them.

And whenever you stand praying, if you have anything against anyone, forgive him, that your Father in heaven may also forgive you your trespasses.

But if you do not forgive, neither will your Father in heaven forgive your trespasses.

Mark 11:22-26

When Jesus and His disciples were leaving Jericho, blind Bartimaeus sat by the road begging. Scripture says that when Bartimaeus **"heard that it was Jesus of Nazareth, he began to cry out and say, 'Jesus, Son of David, have mercy on me!'"** (Mark 10:47). When people told him to be quiet, blind Bartimaeus **"cried out all the more, 'Son of David, have mercy on me!'"** (v. 48).

Blind Bartimaeus got Jesus' attention. Scripture says, **"Jesus stood still and commanded him to be called. Then they called the blind man, saying to him, 'Be of good cheer. Rise, He is calling you'"** (v. 49).

Scripture says that Bartimaeus threw aside his garment, rose, and came to Jesus.

You don't take off your beggar's robe when you're blind unless you don't expect to be a beggar anymore! He took off his beggar's robe and came to Jesus. Jesus said, **"What do you want Me to do for you?"** Bartimaeus said, **"Rabboni, that I may receive my sight"** (v. 51). Jesus said, **"'Go your way; your faith has made you well.' And immediately he received his sight and followed Jesus on the road"** (Mark 10:52).

Bartimaeus didn't spend fifteen minutes describing his

problem. Speak to your mountain without wavering, suspicion, or doubting. If you truly believe something, you will say it because "out **of the abundance of the heart the mouth speaks"** (Matthew 12:34). The mouth reveals what's in the heart. They are connected. One reveals the other. *So you will have what you say when you believe that what you say will come to pass.*

What if Jesus walked up to you and said, "From this point on, whatever you say is going to come to pass"? That would change your life! It's in the red! He has already said it! You've been waiting on it, but He said it 2,000 years ago.

If you are believing and speaking, "I am blessed," and you are walking in obedience to God's Word, then His blessings will overtake you. If you are saying, "Jesus, You're the Lord of my life," and you have corresponding actions with it, then His lordship will rule your life.

What causes a person to believe with his/her heart? It is based upon the Word of God and saying what God has already spoken. That's where the power is. We can base our life on His Word, believe it, receive it, speak it, and live by it.

If someone says to you, "Now, I want you to tell me the truth," you have to establish, *What is truth?* Is truth what you feel? Is it what you see? Is it what the 6:00 news says? John 17:17 says, **"Your word is truth."** Romans 3:4 says, **"Let God be true but every man a liar. . . ."**

Many people speak of having bad days. Instead of speaking "a bad day," begin to say, *This is the day of victory for me. Goodness and mercy are following me every day of my life. Lord, You are my Shepherd, I shall not want. Thank You that You have been made wisdom unto me. I have the mind of Christ. I am blessed coming and I am blessed going. This is the best day of my life!*

You cannot underestimate the importance of guarding the words that are coming out of your mouth as a *lifestyle principle* – not just a one-time thing or a remedy for a crisis!

What you say is coming your way. The seeds of your words are going to grow. What you speak you release. Jesus said, **"Whatever you bind on earth will be bound in heaven, and whatever you loose on earth will be loosed in heaven"** (Matthew 18:18). He is talking about our words.

Angels Respond to the Spoken Word

There is a battle going on in the unseen realm around us, and the angels are coming for our words that are aligned with God's Word. Hebrews 1:14 says that angels are ministering spirits, sent forth to minister for those who will inherit salvation. "Ministering spirits" are servants. That means God's angels are your servants. You are a servant of God as well as a son or a daughter of God. God has commissioned His angels to serve those who are doing His work in the earth. As His child, He has commissioned angels to assist you, guide you, help you, and deliver you.

Psalm 103:20 says, **"Bless the Lord, you His angels, who excel in strength, who do His word, *heeding the voice of His word.*"** When you speak God's Word, the angels are coming to fulfill those words. When you call things that are not as though they were, God begins to bring situations to pass to cause that Word to be fulfilled.

We Framed Our Circumstances with God's Word

When we first started pastoring in Tulsa, in two years we grew from 200 to 300 people to about 2,000. We went to six Sunday services: 8:00, 9:30, 11:00, 1:00, 5:00, and 7:00.

Deuteronomy 6:10,11 says:

"So it shall be, when the Lord your God brings you into the land of which He swore to your fathers, to Abraham, Isaac, and Jacob, to give you large and beautiful cities which you did not build,

"Houses full of all good things, which you did not fill, hewn-out wells which you did not dig, vineyards and olive trees which you did not plant. . . ."

As I read that, I said, "Lord, I'm the seed of Abraham and I have a need."

We moved from one site into a remodeled car dealership. It filled immediately so we moved into a tent. Late that fall, we had to go back into the building for services because of the weather. We ended up turning people away from our church services so we would not violate fire marshal codes.

One Sunday someone brought an unsaved relative to one of our services. Every seat was filled and they were turned away at the door. It's one of those gut-wrenching, painful experiences, and it seemed like there was no way out of this dilemma. We were in a box. We had heard that you could turn your ship around *with the words of your mouth.* You could come out of the hole if you would begin speaking faith (God's Word) and calling those things which were not as though they were.

I said, "Father, I pray in the name of Jesus for buildings that are bigger than we have to put the people and more parking than we need." From that point on, every time I'd start to get worried or harassed about it, I'd say, "Father, I thank You that we have buildings we didn't build and parking lots that we didn't pave."

Today we are holding Sunday services in a beautiful building we didn't build, surrounded by a parking lot we didn't pave. Our services are held in the Mabee Center on the Oral Roberts University campus.

Then we began to confess, "Lord, we thank You for land that we will buy with cash and facilities that we will build with cash." Today that building is located across the street from the O.R.U. campus with classrooms and a gym and auditorium. Now we have services in this building and the Mabee Center.

The same principle worked with our Victory Bible Institute building. The former T. L. and Daisy Osborn World Headquarters building was donated to Victory by the Osborns. This is a 108,000 square foot facility.

Your Words Have Awesome Power

What I am telling you is not something that you're going to confess today and possess by tomorrow. I'm talking about framing your life and the lives of your children and others with the Word of God becoming a way of life.

You see, your words have awesome power. They can cause things to grow inside of you as you nurture them and believe them.

You may have been a dope addict, an alcoholic, or you may have been bombed out in some area of your life, but today you are forgiven, redeemed, and delivered. Begin to say what God says about you.

If you had poverty in your family and you've grown up saying, "We never have enough. Nobody in our family ever went to college," you can live in that box if you want to. But the good news is, *you can get out of that box if you want to.* Jesus can lift you out of any pit that you're in. The key to your freedom is to catch hold of God's Word and begin to believe and speak it, and align your lifestyle with it.

The Centurion Understood the Power of the Spoken Word

In Matthew, chapter 8, a centurion came to Jesus seeking healing for one of his servants. He said, **"Lord, my servant is lying at home paralyzed, dreadfully tormented"** (v. 6). Jesus said, **"I will come and heal him"** (v. 7). The centurion said, **"Lord, I am not worthy that You should come under my roof. *But only speak a word, and my servant will be healed"*** (v. 8). It was Jesus' turn to go, "Wow!" The Bible says Jesus marveled.

Jesus didn't say, "Listen, you're in hyper faith. You've gone overboard and you're stretching the message that I am trying to preach. You've jumped off the deep end with the rest of those charismatics!" No way! Jesus lifted the centurion up on a pedestal forever and said, **"I have not found such great faith, not even in Israel!"** (v. 10).

We are not talking about kindergarten stuff. We are talking about mountain-moving faith in your life. Would you like to rise to that level? How did the centurion step into it? He understood the authority of the spoken Word: **"For I also am a man under authority, having soldiers under me. And I say to this one, 'Go,' and he goes; and to another, 'Come,' and he comes; and to my servant, 'Do this,' and he does it!"** (v. 9). He understood that Jesus' Word had power when it was spoken, and Jesus' healing virtue would heal someone even miles away.

Jesus is telling you and me, "You've got My Word. Speak My Word only and the angels are on their way to perform it in your behalf."

Jesus said to the centurion, **"'Go your way; and as you have believed, so let it be done for you.' And his servant was healed that same hour"** (v. 13).

The Three Hebrew Boys' Words Agreed with God's Word

Think about the three Hebrew boys who stood before Nebuchadnezzar. Let's read this account in Daniel 3:14-28:

Nebuchadnezzar spoke, saying to them, "Is it true, Shadrach, Meshach, and Abednego, that you do not serve my gods or worship the gold image which I have set up?

"Now if you are ready at the time you hear the sound of the horn, flute, harp, lyre, and psaltery, in symphony with all kinds of music, and you fall down and worship the image which I have made, good! But if you do not worship, you shall be cast immediately into the midst of a burning fiery furnace. And who is the god who will deliver you from my hands?"

Shadrach, Meshach, and Abednego answered and said to the king [listen to their words], *"O Nebuchadnezzar, we have no need to answer you in this matter.*

"If that is the case, our God whom we serve is able to deliver us from the burning fiery furnace, and He will deliver us from your hand, O king.

"But if not, let it be known to you, O king, that we do not serve your gods, nor will we worship the gold image which you have set up."

Then Nebuchadnezzar was full of fury, and the expression on his face changed toward Shadrach, Meshach, and Abednego. He spoke and commanded that they heat the furnace seven times more than it was usually heated.

And he commanded certain mighty men of valor who were in his army to bind Shadrach, Meshach, and Abednego, and cast them into the burning fiery furnace.

Then these men were bound in their coats, their

trousers, their turbans, and their other garments, and were cast into the midst of the burning fiery furnace.

Therefore, because the king's command was urgent, and the furnace exceedingly hot, the flame of the fire killed those men who took up Shadrach, Meshach, and Abednego.

And these three men, Shadrach, Meshach, and Abednego, fell down bound into the midst of the burning fiery furnace.

Then King Nebuchadnezzar was astonished; and he rose in haste and spoke, saying to his counselors, "Did we not cast three men bound into the midst of the fire?" They answered and said to the king, "True, O king."

"Look!" he answered, "I see four men loose, walking in the midst of the fire; and they are not hurt, and the form of the fourth is like the Son of God."

Then Nebuchadnezzar went near the mouth of the burning fiery furnace and spoke, saying, "Shadrach, Meshach, and Abednego, servants of the Most High God, come out, and come here." Then Shadrach, Meshach, and Abednego came from the midst of the fire.

And the satraps, administrators, governors, and the king's counselors gathered together, and they saw these men on whose bodies the fire had no power; the hair of their head was not singed nor were their garments affected, and the smell of fire was not on them.

Nebuchadnezzar spoke, saying, "Blessed be the God of Shadrach, Meshach, and Abednego, who sent His Angel and delivered His servants who trusted in Him, and they have frustrated the king's word, and yielded their bodies, that they should not serve nor worship any god except their own God!"

These three Hebrew boys ended up in the fire, but God got in the fire with them. God responded to their words. They said, **"Our God whom we serve is able to deliver us . . . and He will deliver us from your hand, O king"** (Daniel 3:17). They spoke it and it happened.

Speak What God Says!

Joshua 1:8 says:

> This Book of the Law shall not depart from your mouth, but you shall meditate in it day and night, that you may observe to do according to all that is written in it. For then you will make your way prosperous, and then you will have good success.

If you put the Word in your mouth, you are going to be able to do according to what is written in it. Many people say, "Well, when I do it, then I can speak it." That's like telling a horse, "When you turn around, I'm going to grab the reins." Or, like saying to a ship, "When you turn around, then we'll turn the rudder."

You grab the reins first, then the horse turns. You turn the rudder, then the ship turns. And so it is with your mouth. You get your mouth going the right direction, then you can do the Word of God and see a manifestation of God's promises in your life.

It is my prayer that you are grasping this lifestyle principle of believing and speaking God's Word rather than speaking circumstances and challenges.

When you grab hold of the reins of your mouth and start speaking what God says about you, your body will turn around and leave the junk — the drugs, alcohol, immorality, impurity, lack of control, irritation, and such — in the heel dust behind you! Your best days are ahead of you.

PERSONAL PRAYER OF COMMITMENT

Father, I now realize that before I can yield the most unruly member of my body to You, my tongue, I must surrender my life to the lordship of Your Son, Jesus Christ.

I do believe that Jesus was crucified, buried, and resurrected and that in His victory at the cross, He paid the full price with His blood for my sins, sicknesses, poverty, and spiritual death. I renounce every work of darkness and I accept You now, Jesus, as my personal Lord and Savior.

Thank You for baptizing me with Your Holy Spirit, Lord, equipping me to be a bold witness for You and to live a victorious, overcoming life.

I yield my tongue to the control and work of the Holy Spirit, Lord, so that it will speak:

- Life rather than death;
- Prosperity rather than poverty and lack;
- Freedom rather than bondage;
- Edification rather than gossip, slander, and maliciousness;
- Health rather of sickness;

- Wholeness rather than brokenness;

- Comfort rather than grief and sorrow;

- Faith rather than fear;

- Confidence rather than inferiority;

- Acceptance rather than condemnation;

- Victory rather than defeat; and

- Excellence rather than mediocrity.

With the life-giving power of my tongue, I will create an atmosphere which is conducive to obeying the destiny You have prepared for me as well as enjoying the inheritance that You have provided for me.

Thank You for new life, Lord Jesus, so I can make a difference in the earth for Your Kingdom!

_____

(Signature)

_____

(Date)